George Washin~~gton's~~ Narman
Rules of ~~Ci~~
and Decent Behavior

A Most Merry and Illustrated Edition

Adapted and Illustrated by
Chip Cooper

© 2012 by Charles F. Cooper

All rights reserved. No part of this book may be reproduced, stored, or transmitted by any means, whether auditory, graphical, mechanical, or electronic, without written permission of the author, except in the case of brief excerpts used in critical articles and reviews.

Table of Contents

Foreword ……..……..…...i

George Washington's Rules of Civility: A Most Merry and Illustrated Edition ……….…….……….1

Appendix: George Washington's Unabridged Rules of Civility and Decent Behavior ……...…..….111

References and Reading ……………………………………………………………….…….….. 120

About the Editor and Illustrator ………...…………………………………………………….…123

Foreword

No one knows exactly when George Washington sat down to write his 110 *Rules of Civility and Decent Behavior in Company and Conversation*, but it is unlikely it was before 1742 when the young George was ten years old. From the writing itself, which is in a highly elegant script but with some errors and misspellings, a reasonable guess is that Washington was between fourteen and sixteen.

So why did the young aspiring Virginia planter and gentleman undertake such a laborious exercise? Was he writing down the ideals that he thought all proper Georgian (no joke intended) gentlemen should follow? Or was it simply an exercise in penmanship imposed by some hypothetical hired tutor? It is even tempting to speculate that George's mother, Mary Ball Washington, who was a rather difficult woman at the best of times, may have wanted to fix in her son's mind what she considered proper and dutiful filial behavior. However, Mary, who once actually prevented George from accepting a midshipman's commission, was probably not directly involved in assigning her son his daily lessons. Certainly, we have nothing in Washington's hand where he wrote "I will not join the British navy" one hundred times.

Whatever his motives or age, Washington kept the list all his life. It was bequeathed with the rest of his voluminous papers to his nephew and Supreme Court Justice, Bushrod Washington. So the *Rules* must have been more to George than a mere schoolboy exercise.

Bushrod Washington died in 1829, and in 1834 Congress authorized the purchase of Washington's papers. The *Rules*, along with his other documents and correspondence, were kept in the State Department until 1904 when they were transferred to the Library of Congress where the manuscript resides today.

It wasn't until 1888 that the physician and historian, Joseph Merideth Toner, made the full set of the *Rules* available to the general public in a small volume. Unfortunately, some areas of the manuscript had suffered some damage, mostly at the bottom of the pages, damage which Dr. Toner attributed to Mount Vernon's industrious mouse population. But except for these gaps, the 1888 edition was as faithful a transcription of the *Rules* as was possible to publish at the time.

The most recent texts, however, are traceable to the publication in 1890 by Moncure Daniel Conway, a Unitarian minister working both in the United States and in England, and to a volume issued in 1926, which was edited by Charles Moore. Both books provided restorations for the manuscript lacunae, and Moore's work was particularly notable as it also included photographic reproductions of the original manuscript. Although the book was rather small (5 ½" X 8"), the reproductions were of good quality, and for the most part Washington's handwriting is quite legible if the copy is in good condition.

Dr. Toner had originally believed the *Rules* originated from Washington himself, but Reverend Conway found they were, in fact, drawn from a volume titled *Youth's Behaviour or Decencie in Conversation amongst men. Composed in French by grave persons for the Use and benefit of their youth. Now newly translated into English by Francis Hawkins*. Using a copy in the British Museum, Reverend Conway was able to fashion reasonable reconstructions of the missing text, and Charles Moore made his restorations by consulting a copy in the Library of Congress. The editing of the two authors differs somewhat, but Moore seems to have paid more attention to having the restored text fit the gaps in Washington's manuscript.

Francis Hawkins, as the title of his book states, was translating into English a set of French rules of etiquette and polite behavior. The French maxims were first written down by women "pensioners" of the town of La Flèche and were published in 1618 along with a Latin translation supplied by a Jesuit priest, Father Léonard Périn. Other editions followed (including a trilingual volume in Latin, German, and Bohemian published in 1629), and the rules were reissued in 1663 by Pierre de Bresche, who provided a new French translation to replace the rather rustic language of the elderly ladies of La Flèche.

Francis was only a boy (somewhere between eight and twelve years old) when he translated the rules into English, but his father – proud of his young son's achievement – arranged for their publication. That was in 1640. Francis's book was evidently popular since by the eighteenth century there had been multiple reprintings and a circulation that was extensive by the standards of the day. The young George probably did not own the book himself, but he could have borrowed a copy. Alternatively he may have been working from an abridgement provided by someone else.

Naturally the question arises. Did the Father of Our Civility practice what he preached? Well, for the most part he did, or at least he made the effort. People who met Washington remarked on his good manners, and his civility certainly comes through in most of the nearly 20,000 letters he wrote over his lifetime. Washington corresponded in a thoughtful, courteous tone, and he would close virtually all his letters – even to the British officers he was fighting – as "I have the Honor, etc", the "etc" referring to the polite and formulaic "to remain your most obedient and humble servant".

But there were lapses, and when irritated, Washington might forget his rules, particularly when someone questioned his good intentions or integrity. In 1774, Washington received a letter from George Muse, one of his former Virginia militiamen that accused the officers of not keeping an agreement to award land to the veterans of the French and Indian Wars. Washington's reply, written decidedly more in anger than in sorrow, was a lesson in incivility. He called Muse an "ungrateful and dirty fellow" who was drunk when he wrote the "impertinent letter", but that "drunkenness is no excuse for rudeness". Washington added that he had already dealt with the complaints, although they were not of much merit, and because of the tenor of Muse's letter, he regretted doing so. He closed by saying "I do not think you merit the least assistance from [signed] G. Washington". He was certainly not Muse's most obedient and humble servant.

In preparing this edition it soon became clear that George Washington was not writing with the illustrator in mind, and that some of the *Rules* would have to be adapted for length, clarity, and consistency. Liberties were also taken to regularize spelling, punctuation, and, capitalization, liberties to which the General (as he was usually called) hopefully would not have objected. The reader is more than welcome to compare this illustrated edition with the unabridged *Rules* which are provided in the Appendix. Any comments regarding differences of opinion in how the *Rules* could have been better rendered are quite welcome – provided, of course, the remarks, like the *Rules*, are civil.

I have the Honor, etc.

C. F. Cooper, Esq.

George Washington's
Rules of Civility
and Decent Behavior

A Most Merry and Illustrated Edition

Rule #1

Every action done in company ought to be with some sign of respect to those that are present.

Rule #2

When in company, put not your hands to any part of the body, not usually discovered.

Show nothing to your friends that may affright them.

Rule #4

In the presence of others, sing not to yourself with a humming noise, nor drum with your fingers or feet.

Rule #5

If you cough, sneeze, sigh, or yawn, do it not loud but privately.

Rule #6

Sleep not when others speak, sit not when others stand, speak not when you should hold your peace, walk not on when others stop.

Rule #7

Put not off your clothes in the presence of others, nor go out of your chamber half dressed.

Rule #8

It's good manners not to speak louder than ordinary.

Rule #9

Spit not in the fire, especially if there be meat before it.

Rule #10

Keep your feet firm and even without putting one on the other or crossing them.

Rule #11

Shift not yourself in the sight of others nor gnaw your nails.

Rule #12

Bedew no one's face with your spittle by approaching too near when you speak.

Rule #13

If you see vermin as fleas, lice, or ticks upon the clothes of your companions, put them off privately. If they be upon your own clothes return thanks to him who puts them off.

Rule #14

Turn not your back to others, and lean not upon anyone.

Rule #15

Keep your hands and teeth clean, yet without showing any great concern for them.

Rule #16

Do not puff up the cheeks, loll not out the tongue, thrust out the lips, or keep the lips too open or too close.

Rule #17

Be no flatterer, neither play with any that delights not to be played withal.

Rule #18

Come not near the books or writings of another so as to read them unless desired. Also look not nigh when another is writing a letter.

Rule #19

Let your countenance be pleasant, but in serious matters somewhat grave.

Rule #20

The gestures of the body must be suited to the discourse you are upon.

Rule #21

Reproach none for the infirmities of nature, nor delight to put them that have in mind thereof.

Rule #22

Show not yourself glad at the misfortune of another though he were your enemy.

Rule #23

When you see a crime punished, you may be inwardly please, but always show pity to the suffering offender.

Rule #24

Do not laugh too loud or too much at any public spectacle.

Rule #25

Superfluous compliments are to be avoided, yet where due, they are not to be neglected.

Rule #26

In pulling off your hat to persons of distinction, as noblemen, justices, and churchmen, make a reverence, bowing more or less according to the custom.

Rule #27

It is ill manners to bid one more eminent than yourself be covered. Likewise he that makes too much haste to put on his hat does not well.

Rule #28

When you present seats, let it be to every one according to his degree.

Rule #29

When you meet with one of greater quality than yourself, stop and retire, especially if it be at a door.

Rule #30

In walking, place yourself on the left of him whom you desire to honour.

Rule #31

If anyone would give place in his own house, the one ought not to accept it. The other, for fear of making him appear uncivil, ought not to press it.

Rule #32

To one that is your equal or not much inferior, you are to give the chief place in your lodging, but not without acknowledging his own unworthiness.

Rule #33

They that are in dignity or in office have in all places precedency, but while they are young, they ought to respect those that are their equals.

Rule #34

It is good manners to prefer them to whom we speak before ourselves, especially if they be above us.

Rule #35

Let your discourse with men of business be short and comprehensive.

Rule #36

Artificers and persons of low degree ought not to use many ceremonies to lords or others of high degree, but respect and highly honour them.

Rule #37

In speaking to men of quality, do not lean nor look them full in the face, nor approach too near them.

Rule #38

In visiting the sick, do not presently play the physician if you be not knowing therein.

Rule #39

In writing or speaking, give to every person his due title according to his degree and the custom of the place.

Rule #40

Strive not with your superiors in argument, but always submit your judgment to others with modesty.

Rule #41

Undertake not to teach your equal in the art himself professes. It savors of arrogancy.

Rule #42

Let your ceremonies in courtesy be proper to the dignity of his place with whom you converse. For it is absurd to act the same with a clown and a prince.

Rule #43

Do not express joy before one sick or in pain, for that contrary passion will aggravate his misery.

Rule #44

When a man does all he can though it succeeds not well, blame not him that did it.

Rule #45

Being to advise or reprehend anyone, show no sign of choler, but do it with all sweetness and mildness.

Rule #46

Take all admonitions thankfully in what time or place so ever given.

Rule #47

Break no jests that are sharp and biting, and if you deliver anything witty and pleasant, abstain from laughing thereat yourself.

Rule #48

Wherein you reprove another, be unblameable yourself, for example is more prevalent than precepts.

Use no reproachful language against anyone, neither curse nor revile.

Rule #50

Be not hasty to believe flying reports to the disparagement of any.

Wear not your clothes, foul, ripped, or dusty, but see they be brushed once every day at least.

Rule #52

In your apparel be modest and keep to the fashion of your equals with respect to times and places.

Rule #53

Run not in the streets upon the toes nor in a dancing fashion.

Rule #54

Play not the peacock, looking everywhere about you to see if you be well decked.

Rule #55

Eat not in the street nor in the house out of season.

Rule #56

Associate yourself with men of good quality if you esteem your own reputation, for it is better to be alone than in bad company.

Rule #57

In walking with one in company, if he be a man of great quality, walk not with him cheek by jowl but somewhat behind him.

Rule #58

In all causes of passion, admit reason to govern.

Never express anything unbecoming, nor act against the rules moral before your inferiors.

Rule #60

Be not immodest in urging your friends to discover a secret.

Utter not base and frivolous things amongst grave and learned men.

At the table, speak not of melancholy things as death and wounds, and if others mention them, change, if you can, the discourse.

A man ought not to value himself of his achievements or riches.

Break not a jest where none take pleasure in mirth. Deride no man's misfortune, though there seems to be some cause.

Rule #65

Speak not injurious words, neither in jest nor earnestly. Scoff at none although they give occasion.

Rule #66

Be not forward, but friendly and courteous, and be not pensive when it's a time to converse.

Rule #67

Detract not from others.

Rule #68

Go not thither where you know not, whether you shall be welcome or not, and when desired, do it briefly.

Rule #69

If two contend together, take not the part of either unconstrained, and be not obstinate in your own opinion.

Rule #70

Reprehend not the imperfections of others, for that belongs to parents, masters, and superiors.

Rule #71

Gaze not on the marks or blemishes of others, and ask not how they came.

Speak not in an unknown tongue in company, but in your own language, and that as those of quality do, and not as the vulgar.

Rule #73

Pronounce not imperfectly nor bring out your words too hastily but orderly and distinctly.

Rule #74

When another speaks, interrupt him not, nor answer him till his speech be ended.

In the midst of discourse, if a person of quality comes in while you are conversing, it's handsome to repeat what was said before.

Rule #76

While you are talking, point not with your finger at him of whom you discourse, nor approach too near him to whom you talk.

Rule #78

Make no comparisons, and if any of the company be commended for any brave act of virtue, commend not another for the same.

Rule #79

Be not apt to relate news if you know not the truth thereof. In discoursing of things you have heard, name not your author.

Rule #80

Be not tedious in discourse or in reading unless you find the company pleased therewith.

Rule #82

Undertake not what you cannot perform, but be careful to keep your promise.

When you deliver a matter, do it without passion and with discretion, however mean the person be you do it to.

Rule #85

In company of these of higher quality than yourself, speak not until you are asked a question. Then stand upright, put on your hat, and answer in few words.

Let thy bearing be such as becomes a man grave, settled, and attentive, and contradict not at every turn what others say.

Be not tedious in discourse, make not many digressions, nor repeat often the same manner of discourse.

Rule #90

Being set at meat, scratch not, neither spit, cough, or blow your nose except there's a necessity for it.

Make no show of taking great delight in your victuals, feed not with greediness, neither find fault with what you eat.

Entertaining anyone at table, it is decent to present him with meat.

Rule #94

Blow not your broth at table, but stay until it cools of itself.

Rule #95

Put not your meat to your mouth with your knife in your hand, neither spit forth the stones of any fruit pie upon a dish.

It's unbecoming to stoop much to one's meat.

Rule #97

Put not another bit into your mouth until the former be swallowed. Let not your morsels be too big for the jowls.

Rule #98

Drink not, nor talk with your mouth full, neither gaze about you while you are drinking.

Rule #99

Before and after drinking, wipe your lips, breathe not then or ever with too great a noise, for it is uncivil.

Rule #100

Cleanse not your teeth with the tablecloth, napkin, fork, or knife, but if others do it, let it be done with a toothpick.

Rule #101

Rinse not your mouth in the presence of others.

Rule #102

It is out of use to call upon the company often to eat, nor need you drink to others every time you drink.

Rule #103

In company, lay not your arm, but only your hand upon the table.

Rule #104

It belongs to the chiefest in company to unfold his napkin and fall to meat first.

Rule #105

At table whatever happens, put on a cheerful countenance, especially if there be strangers. For good humour makes one dish of meat a feast.

Rule #106

Set not yourself at the upper of the table, but if it be your due or that the master of the house will have it so, contend not, lest you should trouble the company.

Rule #107

If others talk at table, be attentive, but talk not with meat in your mouth.

Rule #108

When you speak of God or his attributes, let it be seriously and with reverence.

Rule #109

Let your recreations be manful, not sinful.

Rule #110

Labor to keep alive in your breast that little spark of celestial fire called conscience.

Appendix

George Washington's Unabridged Rules of Civility and Decent Behavior

The version of George Washington's *Rules of Civility and Decent Behavior* given below is unabridged except in matters of spelling, punctuation, capitalization, – and, yes, of errors. Restorations were based on *Youth's Behaviour or Decency in Conversation* by Francis Hawkins and are therefore at times and by necessity educated guesses. But otherwise, the *Rules* have been kept to those as written by the youthful George Washington.

1. Every action done in company ought to be with some sign of respect to those that are present.
2. When in company, put not your hands to any part of the body, not usually discovered.
3. Show nothing to your friend that may affright him.
4. In the presence of others, sing not to yourself with a humming noise, nor drum with your fingers or feet.
5. If you cough, sneeze, sigh, or yawn, do it not loud but privately, and speak not in your yawning, but put your handkerchief or hand before your face and turn aside.
6. Sleep not when others speak, sit not when others stand, speak not when you should hold your peace, walk not on when others stop.
7. Put not off your clothes in the presence of others, nor go out of your chamber half dressed.
8. At play and at fire it's good manners to give place to the last comer and affect not to speak louder than ordinary.
9. Spit not in the fire, nor stoop low before it. Neither put your hands into the flames to warm them, nor set your feet upon the fire, especially if there be meat before it.
10. When you sit down, keep your feet firm and even without putting one on the other or crossing them.

11. Shift not yourself in the sight of others nor gnaw your nails.
12. Shake not the head, feet, or legs, roll not the eyes, lift not one eyebrow higher than the other, wry not the mouth, and bedew no man's face with your spittle by approaching too near him when you speak.
13. Kill no vermin as fleas, lice, ticks, etc., in the sight of others. If you see any filth or thick spittle, put your foot dexterously upon it. If it be upon the clothes of your companions, put it off privately, and if it be upon your own clothes, return thanks to him who puts it off.
14. Turn not your back to others especially in speaking, jog not the table or desk on which another reads or writes. Lean not upon any one.
15. Keep your nails clean and short, also your hands and teeth clean, yet without showing any great concern for them.
16. Do not puff up the cheeks, loll not out the tongue, rub the hands or beard, thrust out the lips, or bite them, or keep the lips too open or too close.
17. Be no flatterer, neither play with any that delights not to be played withal.
18. Read no letters, books, or papers in company, but when there is a necessity for the doing of it, you must ask leave. Come not near the books or writings of another so as to read them unless desired, or give your opinion of them unasked. Also look not nigh when another is writing a letter.
19. Let your countenance be pleasant, but in serious matters somewhat grave.
20. The gestures of the body must be suited to the discourse you are upon.
21. Reproach none for the infirmities of nature, nor delight to put them that have in mind thereof.
22. Show not yourself glad at the misfortune of another though he were your enemy.
23. When you see a crime punished, you may be inwardly pleased, but always show pity to the suffering offender.
24. Do not laugh too loud or too much at any public spectacle lest you cause yourself to be laughed at.
25. Superfluous compliments and all affectation of ceremony are to be avoided, yet where due, they are not to be neglected.

26. In pulling off your hat to persons of distinction, as noblemen, justices, churchmen, etc., make a reverence, bowing more or less according to the custom of the better bred and quality of the person. Amongst your equals expect not always that they should begin with you first, but to pull off the hat when there is no need is affectation. In the manner of saluting and resaluting in words, keep to the most usual custom.
27. It is ill manners to bid one more eminent than yourself be covered, as well as not to do it to whom it's due. Likewise he that makes too much haste to put on his hat does not well, yet he ought to put it on at the first, or at most, the second time of being asked. Now what is herein spoken of qualification in behaviour in saluting ought also to be observed in taking of place, and sitting down for ceremonies without bounds is troublesome.
28. If anyone comes to speak to you while you are sitting, stand up though he be your inferior, and when you present seats, let it be to every one according to his degree.
29. When you meet with one of greater quality than yourself, stop and retire, especially if it be at a door or any straight place to give way for him to pass.
30. In walking, the highest place in most countries seems to be on the right hand. Therefore place yourself on the left of him whom you desire to honour. But if three walk together, the middle place is the most honourable, and the wall is usually given to the most worthy if two walk together.
31. If anyone far surpasses others, either in age, estate, or merit, yet would give place to a meaner than himself in his own house or elsewhere, the one ought not to accept it. So the other for fear of making him appear uncivil ought not to press it above once or twice.
32. To one that is your equal or not much inferior, you are to give the chief place in your lodging, and he to whom it is offered ought at the first to refuse it, but at the second to accept, though not without acknowledging his own unworthiness.
33. They that are in dignity or in office have in all places precedency, but while they are young, they ought to respect those that are their equals in birth or other qualities, though they have no public charge.

34. It is good manners to prefer them to whom we speak before ourselves, especially if they be above us with whom in no sort we ought to begin.
35. Let your discourse with men of business be short and comprehensive.
36. Artificers and persons of low degree ought not to use many ceremonies to lords or others of high degree, but respect and highly honour them, and those of high degree ought to treat them with affability and courtesy without arrogancy.
37. In speaking to men of quality, do not lean nor look them full in the face, nor approach too near them. At least keep a full pace from them.
38. In visiting the sick, do not presently play the physician if you be not knowing therein.
39. In writing or speaking, give to every person his due title according to his degree and the custom of the place.
40. Strive not with your superiors in argument, but always submit your judgment to others with modesty.
41. Undertake not to teach your equal in the art himself professes. It savors of arrogancy.
42. Let your ceremonies in courtesy be proper to the dignity of his place with whom you converse. For it is absurd to act the same with a clown and a prince.
43. Do not express joy before one sick or in pain, for that contrary passion will aggravate his misery.
44. When a man does all he can though it succeeds not well, blame not him that did it.
45. Being to advise or reprehend anyone, consider whether it ought to be in public or in private, presently, or at some other time in what terms to do it, and in reproving show no sign of choler, but do it with all sweetness and mildness.
46. Take all admonitions thankfully in what time or place so ever given, but afterwards, not being culpable, take a time and place convenient to let him know it that gave them.
47. Mock not nor jest at anything of importance. Break no jests that are sharp and biting, and if you deliver anything witty and pleasant, abstain from laughing thereat yourself.

48. Wherein you reprove another, be unblameable yourself, for example is more prevalent than precepts.
49. Use no reproachful language against anyone, neither curse nor revile.
50. Be not hasty to believe flying reports to the disparagement of any.
51. Wear not your clothes, foul, ripped, or dusty, but see they be brushed once every day at least, and take heed that you approach not to any uncleanness.
52. In your apparel be modest and endeavour to accommodate nature, rather than to procure admiration. Keep to the fashion of your equals such as are civil and orderly with respect to times and places.
53. Run not in the streets, neither go too slowly nor with mouth open. Walk without striking the ground too hard and not upon the toes, nor in a dancing fashion.
54. Play not the peacock, looking everywhere about you to see if you be well decked, if your shoes fit well, if your stockings sit neatly and clothes handsomely.
55. Eat not in the street nor in the house out of season.
56. Associate yourself with men of good quality if you esteem your own reputation, for it is better to be alone than in bad company.
57. In walking up and down in a house only with one in company, if he be greater than yourself, at the first give him the right hand and stop not until he does, and be not the first that turns, and when you do turn, let it be with your face towards him. If he be a man of great quality, walk not with him cheek by jowl but somewhat behind him, but yet in such a manner that he may easily speak to you.
58. Let your conversation be without malice or envy, for it is a sign of a tractable and commendable nature, and in all causes of passion, admit reason to govern.
59. Never express anything unbecoming, nor act against the rules moral before your inferiors.
60. Be not immodest in urging your friends to discover a secret.
61. Utter not base and frivolous things amongst grave and learned men, nor very difficult questions or subjects among the ignorant, or things hard to be believed. Stuff not your discourse with sentences amongst your betters nor equals.

62. Speak not of doleful things in a time of mirth or at the table. Speak not of melancholy things as death and wounds, and if others mention them, change, if you can, the discourse. Tell not your dreams, but to your intimate friend.
63. A man ought not to value himself of his achievements or rare qualities, high birth, dignities, riches, virtue, or kindred.
64. Break not a jest where none take pleasure in mirth. Laugh not aloud, nor at all without occasion. Deride no man's misfortune, though there seems to be some cause.
65. Speak not injurious words, neither in jest nor earnestly. Scoff at none although they give occasion.
66. Be not forward, but friendly and courteous, the first to salute, hear, and answer, and be not pensive when it's a time to converse.
67. Detract not from others. Neither be excessive in commending.
68. Go not thither where you know not, whether you shall be welcome or not. Give not advice without being asked, and when desired, do it briefly.
69. If two contend together, take not the part of either unconstrained, and be not obstinate in your own opinion. In things indifferent, be of the major side.
70. Reprehend not the imperfections of others, for that belongs to parents, masters, and superiors.
71. Gaze not on the marks or blemishes of others, and ask not how they came. What you may speak in secret to your friend, deliver not before others.
72. Speak not in an unknown tongue in company, but in your own language, and that as those of quality do, and not as the vulgar. Sublime matters treat seriously.
73. Think before you speak. Pronounce not imperfectly nor bring out your words too hastily but orderly and distinctly.
74. When another speaks, be attentive yourself and disturb not the audience. If any hesitate in his words, help him not nor prompt him without desired. Interrupt him not, nor answer him until his speech be ended.

75. In the midst of discourse, ask not of what it is about, but if you perceive any stops because of your arrival, rather request the speaker to proceed. If a person of quality comes in while you are conversing, it's handsome to repeat what was said before.
76. While you are talking, point not with your finger at him of whom you discourse, nor approach too near him to whom you talk, especially to his face.
77. Treat with men at fit times about business, and whisper not in the company of others.
78. Make no comparisons, and if any of the company be commended for any brave act of virtue, commend not another for the same.
79. Be not apt to relate news if you know not the truth thereof. In discoursing of things you have heard, name not your author. Always a secret discover not.
80. Be not tedious in discourse or in reading unless you find the company pleased therewith.
81. Be not curious to know the affairs of others, neither approach those that speak in private.
82. Undertake not what you cannot perform, but be careful to keep your promise.
83. When you deliver a matter, do it without passion and with discretion, however mean the person be you do it to.
84. When your superiors talk to anybody, hearken not, neither speak nor laugh.
85. In company of these of higher quality than yourself, speak not until you are asked a question. Then stand upright, put on your hat, and answer in few words.
86. In disputes be not so desirous to overcome as not to give liberty to each one to deliver his opinion, and submit to the judgment of the major part, especially if they are judges of the dispute.
87. Let thy bearing be such as becomes a man grave, settled, and attentive to what is said without being too serious. Contradict not at every turn what others say.
88. Be not tedious in discourse, make not many digressions, nor repeat often the same manner of discourse.
89. Speak not evil of the absent, for it is unjust.
90. Being set at meat, scratch not, neither spit, cough, or blow your nose except there's a necessity for it.

91. Make no show of taking great delight in your victuals, feed not with greediness, cut your bread with a knife, lean not on the table, neither find fault with what you eat.
92. Take no salt or cut bread with your knife greasy.
93. Entertaining anyone at table, it is decent to present him with meat. Undertake not to help others undesired by the master.
94. If you soak bread in the sauce, let it be no more than what you put in your mouth at a time, and blow not your broth at table, but stay until it cools of itself.
95. Put not your meat to your mouth with your knife in your hand, neither spit forth the stones of any fruit pie upon a dish, nor cast anything under the table.
96. It's unbecoming to stoop much to one's meat. Keep your fingers clean, and when foul, wipe them on a corner of your table napkin.
97. Put not another bit into your mouth until the former be swallowed. Let not your morsels be too big for the jowls.
98. Drink not, nor talk with your mouth full, neither gaze about you while you are drinking.
99. Drink not too leisurely nor yet too hastily. Before and after drinking, wipe your lips, breathe not then or ever with too great a noise, for it is uncivil.
100. Cleanse not your teeth with the tablecloth, napkin, fork, or knife, but if others do it, let it be done with a pick tooth.
101. Rinse not your mouth in the presence of others.
102. It is out of use to call upon the company often to eat, nor need you drink to others every time you drink.
103. In company of your betters, be not longer in eating than they are. Lay not your arm, but only your hand upon the table.
104. It belongs to the chiefest in company to unfold his napkin and fall to meat first. But he ought then to begin in time and to dispatch with dexterity that the slowest may have time allowed him.

105. Be not angry at table whatever happens, and if you have reason to be so, show it not, but put on a cheerful countenance, especially if there be strangers. For good humour makes one dish of meat a feast.
106. Set not yourself at the upper of the table, but if it be your due or that the master of the house will have it so, contend not, lest you should trouble the company.
107. If others talk at table, be attentive, but talk not with meat in your mouth.
108. When you speak of God or his attributes, let it be seriously and with reverence. Honor and obey your natural parents although they be poor.
109. Let your recreations be manful, not sinful.
110. Labor to keep alive in your breast that little spark of celestial fire called conscience.

References and Reading

Early Print Editions

Washington's rules of civility and decent behavior in company and conversation. A paper found among the early writings of George Washington. Copied from the original with literal exactness, and edited with notes, J. M. Toner, M. D. (Ed.), W. H Morrison (1888). This was the first full publication of George Washington's *Rules of Civility*. Gaps are indicated by dots and the original spelling, punctuation, and capitalization are retained.

George Washington's Rules of Civility Traced to Their Sources and Restored, Moncure D. Conway (Ed.), John W. Lovell Company (1890). The original French maxims and the English translation by Francis Hawkins are printed along with each of Washington's rules. This was the first edition to provide reliable restorations.

George Washington's Rules of Civility and Decent Behaviour in Company and Conversation, Charles Moore (Ed.), Houghton Mifflin (1926). This volume contains both a transcription and photographic reproductions of the original manuscript, as well as the corresponding rules found in Hawkins. Restorations are indicated in brackets. Although the book is small, the manuscript reproductions are generally legible.

Internet Resources

Internet addresses tend to be changeable, disappear, and may remain accessible even though they are no longer being actively maintained. But at the time of this writing the following websites have additional information about George Washington's *Rules of Civility*.

The Papers of George Washington (University of Virginia). Washington's Copy of Rules of Civility & Decent Behaviour In Company and Conversation, http://gwpapers.virginia.edu/documents/civility/index.html This site has a complete transcription of the *Rules* along with the manuscript facsimile. In the transcriptions, restored words and passages are indicated by brackets, but words and spelling are as close to the original writing as can be determined. An excellent on-line edition.

The website itself at http://gwpapers.virginia.edu/ has numerous documents from and relating to George Washington, including an excellent selection of articles by knowledgeable experts. Of particular interest is a modern medical assessment of George Washington's last illness, convincingly argued to be acute epiglottitis. The full account of Washington's death, including the first hand account of his Mount Vernon manager, Tobias Lear, is especially worth reading.

The Writings of George Washington from the Original Manuscript Sources, 1745 – 1799, http://etext.virginia.edu/washington/fitzpatrick/ An online edition from the University of Virginia of John Fitzpatrick's 1938 edition of Washington's manuscripts which included over 17,000 letters. The site is searchable and is a good resource for the beginning Washington scholar.

Other Reading

Washington: A Life, Ron Chernow, Penguin (2010)

The Unexpected George Washington: His Private Life, Harlow Giles Unger, Wiley (2006).

Realistic Visionary: A Portrait of George Washington, Peter Henriques, University of Virginia Press (2006)

His Excellency: George Washington, Joseph Ellis, Knopf (2004)

An Imperfect God: George Washington, His Slaves, and the Creation of America, Henry Wiencek, Straus and Diroux (2003).

George Washington and Slavery: A Documentary Portrayal, Fritz Hirschfeld, University of Missouri (1997).

Washington, the Indispensible Man, James Thomas Flexner, Collins (1974)

"Washington Takes Charge", Joseph Ellis, *Smithsonian Magazine,* January 2005.

About the Editor and Illustrator

Although he is not first in war, first in peace, and certainly not first in the hearts of his countrymen, Charles F. "Chip" Cooper became an admirer of George Washington when he first read the stories that George threw a silver dollar across the Potomac, had wooden teeth, and chopped down his father's cherry tree, none of which are true. But even after he began reading

stories about George that *were* true, he found there was still much to admire in Washington's life and character, not the least the General's desire to always behave in a manner courteous, dignified, and civil. It is hoped that this Most Merry and Illustrated Edition of *George Washington's Rules of Civility and Decent Behavior* will stand as a small tribute to the first and most civil of America's Founding Fathers.

    A previous book by the same author, *A Most Merry and Illustrated History of the Last Days of Pompeii*, is also available.

Made in the USA
Coppell, TX
17 January 2020